Mammals

Reviewed by Bill Houska, D.V.M.,
Ridgemont Animal Hospital, Rochester, New York,
and James K. Morrisey, D.V.M., Cornell University
School of Veterinary Medicine.

Debra J. Housel

Table of Contents

Scientists have found more than 4,550 kinds of mammals.

◀ beaver

What Is a Mammal?

They come in many shapes and sizes. They may swim in oceans or run through deserts and fields. Some climb trees or cliffs. They live in rain forests, frozen places, or even in your home. What are they? Mammals.

There is at least one mammal living in your home. You! Humans are mammals.

▲ Orca
(killer whale)

Mammals are warm-blooded animals. They are called *vertebrates* (VER-tuh-brits) because they have backbones.

Being warm-blooded means that a mammal's body stays the same *temperature* all of the time. In order to do this, a mammal must eat lots of food. It also has hair, fur, or a layer of fat to keep it warm. Sometimes it has more than one of these. A polar bear has both thick fur and fat because it lives where it's always cold.

A rabbit's body stays 102°F all the time. ▶

Smart!

Mammals have the biggest and smartest brains of all animals. People often choose mammals for pets because they can be trained. If you have a dog, cat, or guinea pig, you have a pet mammal.

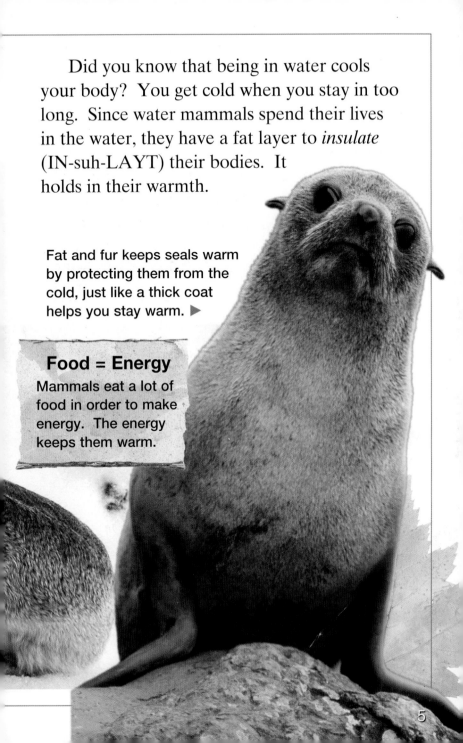

Did you know that being in water cools your body? You get cold when you stay in too long. Since water mammals spend their lives in the water, they have a fat layer to *insulate* (IN-suh-LAYT) their bodies. It holds in their warmth.

Fat and fur keeps seals warm by protecting them from the cold, just like a thick coat helps you stay warm. ▶

Food = Energy
Mammals eat a lot of food in order to make energy. The energy keeps them warm.

Some mammals, like whales, live in the sea. Others live on land. Land mammals have four *limbs.* No matter where they live, all mammals breathe with their lungs.

All water mammals must come to the surface to breathe. ▶

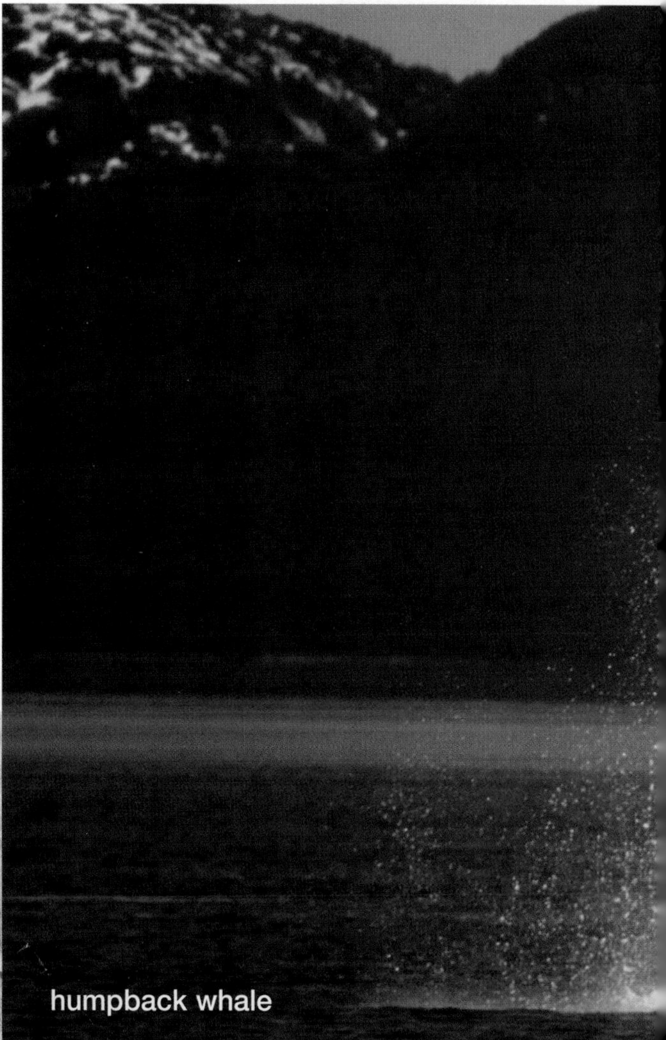

humpback whale

What Is It?
A land mammal's **limbs** are its legs and arms.

Male and female mammals must mate in order to have *offspring*. Most mammal babies grow inside their mothers. The mothers give birth to live young. The young are born helpless, so they need a parent's care. They must drink their mothers' milk. It may take weeks or years before they can fend for themselves. Just think of how long it will take you to grow up!

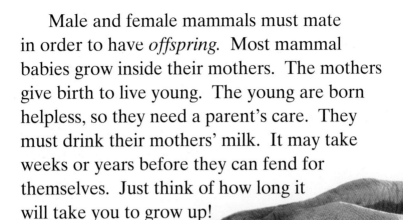

Some mammals such as elephants take a long time to grow up. ▶

Offspring
The offspring of an animal are its babies. Babies come from, or "spring off," their parents.

The time a mother mammal carries her babies before giving birth is called *gestation* (je-STAY-shuhn). The number of days is different for each *species* (SPEE-sheez or SPEE-seez).

Mammal	Number of Days of Gestation
African elephant	660
camel	390
human	280
cow	270
fruit bat	180
pig	114
chinchilla	111
lion	100
beaver	90
wolf	63
rabbit	30
gerbil	26

What Is It?

A **species** is an animal group such as cats, dogs, rabbits, or bears. A species can also be a plant group such as roses, daisies, or pine trees.

Kinds of Mammals

Scientists group mammals by the things they have in common. One group, *primates,* is the species name for humans, apes, and monkeys. Most primates have thumbs. Thumbs let primates grab and pick up things. Primates are *omnivores* (OM-nuh-vohrs) because they can eat both plants and animals.

▲ a baby Bornean orangutan

10

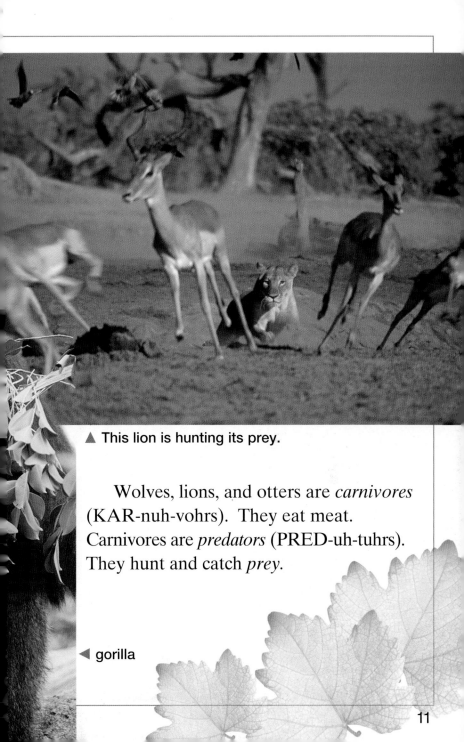

▲ This lion is hunting its prey.

Wolves, lions, and otters are *carnivores* (KAR-nuh-vohrs). They eat meat. Carnivores are *predators* (PRED-uh-tuhrs). They hunt and catch *prey*.

◄ gorilla

How are deer, giraffes, and cows alike? They have hoofs. Hoofed mammals are *herbivores* (HUR-buh-vohrs), which means they eat only plants. The larger the animal, the more plants it must eat.

Most mammals have jaws and teeth. *Rodents* and rabbits have front teeth that grow

▲ Zebras are herbivores.

constantly. They must chew hard things like tree bark to keep their teeth from becoming too long.

Do you have a pet rodent? You do if you have a mouse, gerbil, or hamster.

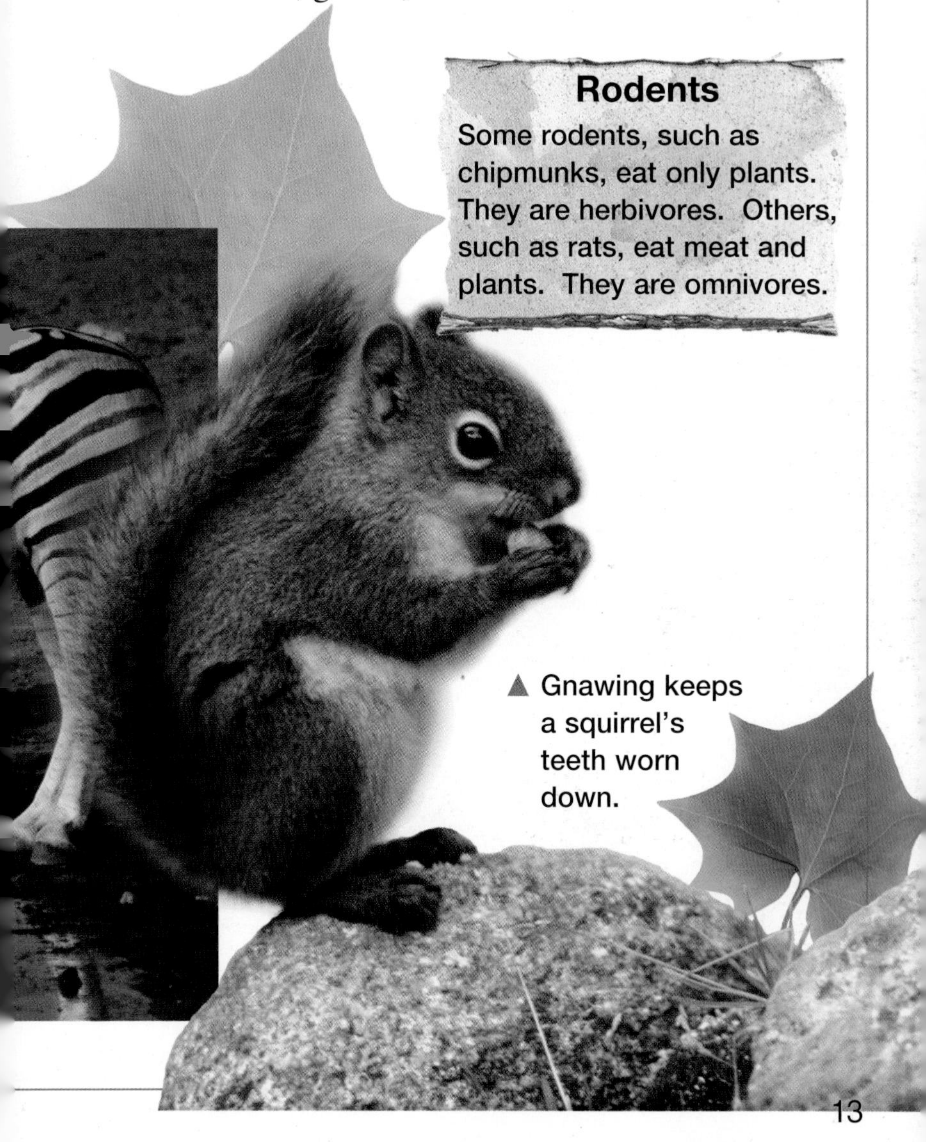

Rodents

Some rodents, such as chipmunks, eat only plants. They are herbivores. Others, such as rats, eat meat and plants. They are omnivores.

▲ Gnawing keeps a squirrel's teeth worn down.

Odd Mammals

Odd mammals are different from all others. For example, anteaters have no teeth. Instead they have long *snouts* and catch bugs with their sticky tongues. They swallow them whole.

All mammals can move. People walk, bears climb, kangaroos jump, and whales swim. But just one mammal can fly. It's a bat!

▲ There are about 1,000 different kinds of bats.

▼ Anteaters love to eat ants. Would you?

Not Really Flying

Flying squirrels may look like they can fly, but they can't. They just control how they fall by gliding.

Marsupials (mar-SOO-pee-uhls) are another group of unusual mammals. They give birth to babies that are alive but not ready to survive apart from their mothers. Each baby must live for weeks or months in its mother's pouch. Many marsupials, including the kangaroo, live in Australia.

◀ tree kangaroo

▲ Marsupial babies stay in their mother's pouch. ▶

Eastern grey kangaroo ▶

Australia and a few nearby islands are the home of the strangest mammals of all. They are called *monotremes* (MON-uh-treems). What makes them so strange? They lay eggs!

The platypus lays its eggs in a nest. After ten days the babies hatch. The mother lies on her back. The babies lick up the milk that oozes from a gland on the surface of her belly. Her milk flows for about two months.

The other mammal that lays eggs is the echidna.

Why Are They Mammals?

Monotremes are called mammals because mammals are the only animals that provide milk for their young.

▲ Platypuses are monotremes.

Lifespans and Habitats

Different mammals can live for different lengths of time. This graph shows the number of years each kind of animal normally lives. Most members of the species die by the age given. A few live longer.

Animal Lifespans

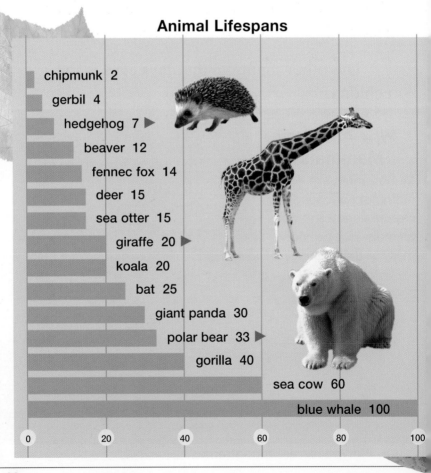

Animal	Lifespan
chipmunk	2
gerbil	4
hedgehog	7 ▶
beaver	12
fennec fox	14
deer	15
sea otter	15
giraffe	20 ▶
koala	20
bat	25
giant panda	30
polar bear	33 ▶
gorilla	40
sea cow	60
blue whale	100

0   20   40   60   80   100

Mammals live in *habitats* all over the world. Because they are warm-blooded, their bodies stay the right temperature no matter where they live. Some mammals live in deserts while others live in a snowy wilderness. How can this be? Each mammal has body features *suited* to where it lives.

The fennec fox and the camel live in the desert. Both can live for days without drinking water. The fennec fox's large ears let extra heat leave its body to keep it from getting too hot.

The musk ox and the Arctic hare live where it gets very cold in the winter. It never gets hot there, even in the summer. They have heavy fur to protect them from the cold.

No Water?

How can some animals go days without drinking water? Fennec foxes can get water from the food they eat. Camels can store large amounts of water in their bodies—but not in their humps, as many people believe.

Fennec fox ▶

Monkeys live in rain forests where it's always hot and *humid*. Chinchillas live on mountains. Whales live in salt water. Some sea cows live in fresh water. You can find mammals almost everywhere!

▲ A chinchilla's thick fur lets it live high on cold mountains.

Some mammals live where there are big changes between the seasons. These animals must survive the heat of summer. They must also survive the bitter cold of winter. Many animals spend the winters *hibernating.*

During the warm months, these animals eat all the food they can find. This builds a layer of fat in their bodies. When it gets cold, they go into a cave or a hole in the ground. They fall asleep, and their heart and lungs slow down. They look dead, but they're fine. Their bodies live on their stored fat. When spring comes, they awaken.

Desert rats do something similar, except they sleep during the hottest, driest season. Then, they are active during the cooler times of the year. Sleeping during the summer is called *aestivation* (es-tuh-VAY-shuhn).

◀ Some mammals hibernate during the winter.

◀ red pandas

As you can see, mammals are very interesting creatures. Aren't you glad to be one?

tarsier ▶

▲ orangutan

Glossary

aestivation to spend the summer in a resting state

carnivores animals that eat only meat

gestation the amount of time a mammal spends developing inside its mother

habitats the places where animals live in nature

herbivores animals that eat only plants

hibernating spending the winter in a resting state

humid moist

insulate to keep heat from escaping

limbs the body parts that stick out from an animal's main body and are used to move or grasp things; on humans these are the arms and legs

marsupials mammals that have a pouch in which to carry young

monotremes mammals that lay eggs

odd unusual or strange

offspring the young of an animal or plant

omnivores animals that eat both plants and meat

predators animals that hunt, kill, and eat other animals

prey any animal that is hunted and eaten by another animal

primates the group of mammals that have hands (usually with thumbs) instead of paws

rodents a group of mammals with four limbs and sharp front teeth that grow all the time

snouts especially long noses

species a group of animals (and plants, too) that are like each other, such as cats, dogs, bears, or humans

suited fitting or made for

temperature an amount of heat measured by a thermometer

vertebrates animals that have spines (backbones)

young babies; animals before they become adults

Index